Attract and Repel
A Look at Magnets

Jennifer Boothroyd

Lerner Publications Company

Minneapolis

To Joe, Jack, and Grace

Tips from the Author on Working with Magnets:

- Remember not to drop or hit magnets.
- Never use magnets near computers, TVs, stereos, or credit cards.
- Always wash your hands after experimenting with magnets.
- Be sure to store magnets in pairs, with their opposite poles touching.

Lerner Publications Company
A division of Lerner Publishing Group, Inc.
241 First Avenue North
Minneapolis, MN 55401 U.S.A.

Website address: www.lernerbooks.com

Library of Congress Cataloging-in-Publication Data

Boothroyd, Jennifer, 1972–
    Attract and repel : a look at magnets / by Jennifer Boothroyd.
        p.   cm. — (Lightning bolt books™—Exploring Physical Science)
    Includes index.
    ISBN 978–0–7613–5429–1 (lib. bdg. : alk. paper)
    1. Magnetism—Juvenile literature. I. Title.
QC753.7.B66 2011
538—dc22   2009047431

Manufactured in the United States of America
1 — BP — 7/15/10

Contents

Magnets Stick

Drawings. A lunch menu. Photos. Many people have things on their refrigerators. But what makes them stick?

Magnets!

A magnet is an object
that sticks to some metals.
Some magnets are natural.
Lodestone is a natural magnet.
Lodestone is a kind of mineral.

Metal nails stick to this
piece of lodestone.

Most magnets are made by people. Man-made magnets come in many shapes and sizes.

Man-made magnets can be shaped like horseshoes, discs, or bars. They come in other shapes too.

A magnet attracts only certain kinds of metals.

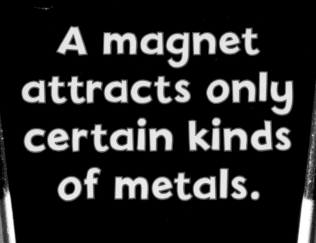

A magnet sticks to this metal. But magnets will not stick to all metals.

A magnet sticks
to steel.

A magnet
sticks to iron.

8

Magnets do not stick to aluminum. They do not stick to copper.

These copper bits are not attracted to the magnet. But the steel bits above them are.

9

Magnets do not stick to wood, cloth, or plastic either.

Magnetic Force

A magnet can move an object without touching it. Magnets move objects through magnetic force.

The force is invisible. You cannot see it.

Magnetic force makes this metal ball move.

Hold a magnet above a steel
paper clip. The paper clip will
fly off the table. It will stick
to the magnet.

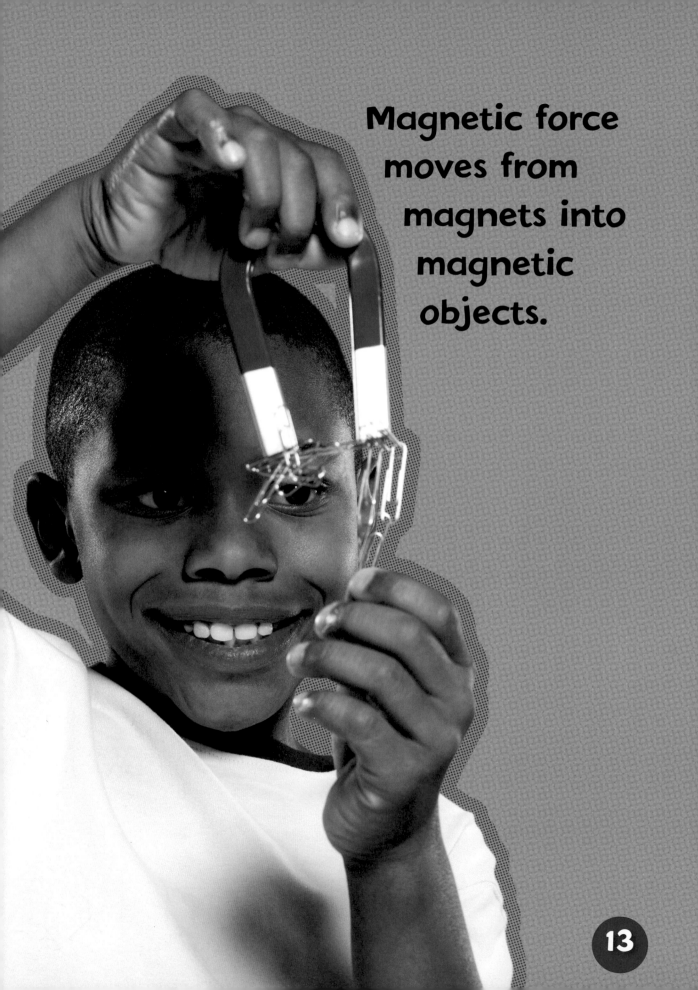

Magnetic force moves from magnets into magnetic objects.

13

Magnetic force can move from one magnetic object to another. It can move into magnetic objects that aren't even touching the magnet!

The paper clips at the end of this chain aren't touching the magnet. But magnetic force moved into them through the clips at the top of the chain.

Magnetic force can pass through nonmagnetic materials. That's how magnets stick to this fridge. The force travels through the white plastic coating and attracts the metal underneath.

Magnetic force can pass through plastic as long as the plastic isn't too thick.

Magnetic force can pass through many materials, such as glass, paper, and cloth.

Magnetic force is passing through this paper. It's attracting the magnet to the metal locker.

Magnetic Poles

Magnets have two poles. The poles are at the ends of a magnet. There is a north pole and a south pole.

The south pole of this magnet is on the left. The north pole is on the right.

Put a magnet in a bowl of steel wool clippings. Most of the metal bits will stick to the ends. A magnet's force is strongest at the poles.

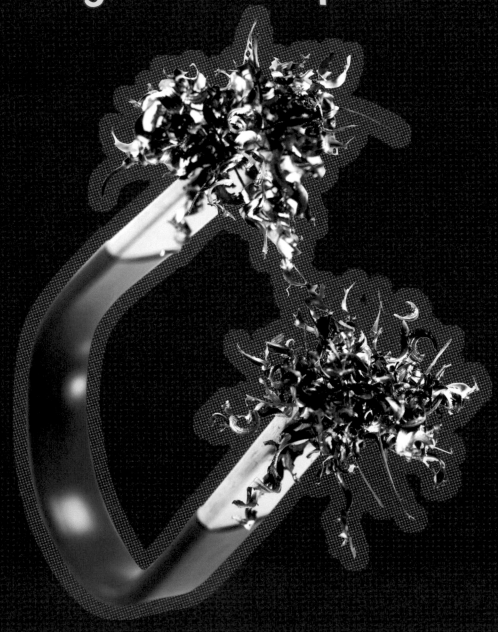

What happens when you put two magnets next to each other? If two south poles or two north poles get too close, they push each other away. **They repel each other.**

The south poles of these magnets are close to each other. The magnets repel each other.

If opposite poles are close, the magnets move together. They attract each other.

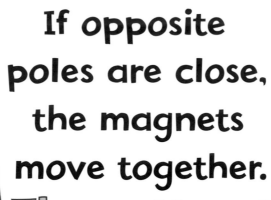

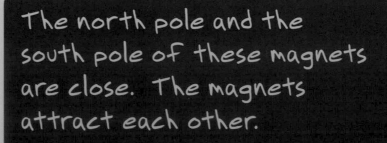

The north pole and the south pole of these magnets are close. The magnets attract each other.

Magnetic Earth

Earth is like a giant magnet. It has a North Pole and a South Pole.

North Pole

South Pole

People learned that a magnet's north pole points toward the North Pole of Earth. Inventors used this information to make the compass.

A compass needle has a magnetic force. It points north.

These boys use a compass to tell them which way is north.

How We use Magnets

People use magnets in many ways. Magnets keep refrigerator doors closed.

Magnets in this refrigerator door help the door stay closed.

They are used in speakers and earbuds. They are also found inside computers.

Giant magnets are used to make electricity. And this train uses powerful magnets to float above its track.

People have found many ways to use a magnet's force. How do you think magnets will be used in the future?

Activity

A Floating Paper Clip

You've probably seen a balloon float in the air. But what about a paper clip? Paper clips need a little help to float. Here's how to make it happen.

What you need:

a scissors
clear nylon thread
a steel paper clip
clear tape
a table
different-sized magnets

What you do:

1. Cut a piece of thread about 6 inches (15 centimeters) long.

2. Tie one end of the thread to the paper clip. Tape the other end to the table.

3. Hold one of the magnets above the paper clip. Slowly raise the magnet so the clip lifts off the table. Keep lifting the magnet until the clip falls back down.

4. Repeat the experiment with each of the different-sized magnets. Which magnets lift the clip the highest in the air?

Glossary

attract: to pull things toward an object. Magnets attract certain kinds of metals.

compass: an instrument for finding directions. Compasses have a magnetic needle that always points north.

force: a push or a pull

lodestone: a mineral that is naturally magnetic

magnet: a piece of metal that attracts iron or steel

nonmagnetic: not attracted by a magnet

opposite: completely different

pole: one of the two opposite ends of a magnet

repel: to push away

Further Reading

Bitesize Science: Magnets and Springs
http://www.bbc.co.uk/schools/ks2bitesize/science/
physical_processes/magnet_springs/read1.shtml

Education World: Strength of Attraction
http://www.educationworld.com/a_lesson/showbiz_
science/showbiz_science017.shtml

Kids' Science Experiments: Magnetism
http://www.kids-science-experiments.com/cat_
magnetic.html

Levine, Shar, and Leslie Johnstone. *Magnet Power!*
New York: Sterling, 2006.

Nelson, Robin. *Magnets.* **Minneapolis: Lerner
Publications Company, 2004.**

Schuh, Mari C. *Magnetism.* **Minneapolis:
Bellwether Media, 2008.**

Index

Photo Acknowledgments

The images in this book are used with the permission of: © Wayne Higgins/Alamy, p. 2; © Tetra Images/Getty Images, p. 4; © Scientifica/Visuals Unlimited, Inc., p. 5; © Newlight/Dreamstime.com, p. 6; © Mike Kemp/Getty Images, pp. 7, 13; © Photolibrary/StockphotoPro.com, p. 8 (bottom); © Iain McGillvray/StockphotoPro.com, p. 8 (top); © Charles D. Winters/Photo Researchers, Inc., p. 9; © iStockphoto.com/Alexandr Makarov, p. 10 (left); © iStockphoto.com/Sze Kit Poon, p. 10 (top right); © iStockphoto.com/Andyd, p. 10 (bottom right); © mauritius images/Photolibrary, p. 11; © John R. Foster/Photo Researchers, Inc., p. 12; © Todd Strand/Independent Picture Service, p. 14; © Antenna/Getty Images, p. 15; © Jeffery Coolidge/CORBIS, p. 16; © ICHIRO/Photodisc/Getty Images, pp. 17, 29 (bottom right); © Tek Image/Photo Researchers, Inc., p. 18; © sciencephotos/Alamy, pp. 19, 20; © Laura Westlund/Independent Picture Service, p. 21; © iStockphoto.com/Luca di Filippo, p. 22; © Moodboard/StockphotoPro.com, p. 23; © Rcmathiraj/Dreamstime.com, p. 24; © Jack Hollingsworth/Photodisc/Getty Images, p. 25; © iStockphoto.com/Nikada, p. 26; NASA, p. 27; © Sonyho/Dreamstime.com, p. 28 (top right); © Coprid/Dreamstime.com, p. 28 (second from top); © Viledevil/ Dreamstime.com, p. 28 (bottom right); © Picturephoto/Dreamstime.com, p. 28 (bottom middle); © Jgroup/Dreamstime.com, p. 29 (top); © iStockphoto.com/Don Nichols (left), p. 29; © Martyn F. Chillmaid/Photo Researchers, Inc., p. 30; © Yiap Edition/Alamy, p. 31.

Front Cover: © Kari Marttila/Alamy